elevenplustutorials.co.uk

11+ English

10-Minute Assessment Tests

Ages
10-11

Spelling, Punctuation and Grammar

**To order further publications visit
elevenplustutorials.co.uk**

© **Jane Armstrong, 2020**

All rights reserved. No part of this book may be reproduced or transmitted in any form or by any means without written permission of the author.

Published : Jane Armstrong, 2020

Contents

	Page		Page
Introduction	4	Test 17	48
Word Definitions	5	Test 18	50
Test 1	6	Test 19	52
Test 2	9	Test 20	55
Test 3	12	Test 21	57
Test 4	15	Test 22	59
Test 5	18	Test 23	62
Test 6	20	Test 24	64
Test 7	23	Test 25	67
Test 8	26	Test 26	69
Test 9	28	Test 27	71
Test 10	31	Test 28	73
Test 11	34	Test 29	75
Test 12	36	Test 30	77
Test 13	39	Test 31	79
Test 14	41	Test 32	81
Test 15	43		
Test 16	46	Answers	83

Introduction

Please read the following carefully before you begin the tests:

- This book contains 32 tests covering a wide variety of spelling, punctuation and grammar questions, a key part of the English requirement in the 11+ examination.

- You should allow 10 minutes for each test. It is wise to get into the habit of limiting the time spent on each test, so do not to exceed 10 minutes. Working to a set time frame is a good way to prepare for the real examination.

- Read each question carefully. Points can easily be lost by misreading a question eg. you may be asked for *reverse* alphabetical order as opposed to alphabetical order.

- Use each question as an opportunity to broaden your vocabulary. Once you have completed a test make a note of any words you may not have heard of before and look them up online or in a dictionary. Also find out if they have an antonym or synonym.

- Good luck and have fun. You will learn more and want to continue learning if you are enjoying yourself.

Word Definitions

This list will help you to understand the words used in this book. You will need to be familiar with these definitions as the words appear regularly in the 11+ examination.

abbreviation	a word or words which are shortened
abstract noun	a word referring to a concept or idea e.g. *anger*
adjective	a word that describes somebody or something
adverb	a word that gives additional meaning to a verb
adverbial phrase	a word or phrase that makes the meaning of a verb, adjective or another adverb more specific e.g. I parked the car *right here*.
alphabetical order	to arrange words according to the English alphabet
antonym	a word that means the opposite of another word
clause	a part of a sentence containing a verb
collective noun	a word that refers to a group e.g *flock* of sheep
compound word	a word formed from two other words e.g. *milkshake*
conjunction	a word used to link sentences, phrases or words e.g. *although, nor*
definition	the meaning of a word
fronted adverbial	an adverbial that has been moved before the verb e.g. *After the rain stopped,* I managed to go to the bank.
main clause	a clause in a sentence that makes sense on its own
metaphor	a way of describing something in a way usually used to describe something else e.g. Zack's teacher was *a dragon!*
modal verb	a verb that changes the meaning of another verb e.g. *could, may*
noun	a word for something or somebody e.g. *table*
past tense	the form of a verb showing that something has already happened
phrase	a small group of words that does not contain a verb e.g. *a sunny day*
plural	a word which represents more than one of something e.g. *bags*
prefix	a group of letters that can be added to the start of a word to change its meaning e.g. *un, dis, non*
preposition	a word that relates other words to each other e.g. the shoes *on* his feet
pronoun	a word used to replace a noun or noun phrase
relative clause	a type of subordinate clause that gives more specificity to the meaning of a noun e.g. the children *who play outside* are noisy
reported speech	what has been said without using speech marks or the exact words
root word	a word that can have a prefix or suffix added to form a new word
singular	a word that means one of something e.g. *bag*
Standard English	the form of English that is widely accepted as the usual form
subordinate clause	this gives more information about the main clause but is dependent upon the main clause and cannot stand alone
suffix	a group of letters that can be added to the end of a word to create a new word e.g. *ion, ity*
synonym	a word with the same or very similar meaning to another word
verb	a 'doing' or 'being' word

Test 1

You have **10** minutes to complete this test

For each line choose the correctly spelt word that completes the sentence.
Circle the letter that corresponds to the correct answer.

1. Thomas eyed everyone **busily** **bisily** **bussily** **bissily** eating their beef and bread
                                      a.   b.   c.   d.

2. and wondered if **dessertt** **dessert** **desert** **desertt** would be served soon. He had
                           a.   b.   c.   d.

3. not eaten since yesterday and his **stumack** **stomack** **stomach** **stumach**
                                           a.   b.   c.   d.

4. rumbled loudly. His **farther** **father** **farfer** **phather** frowned at him.
                       a.   b.   c.   d.

5. Which of the following words is spelt correctly?
   Circle the letter that corresponds to the correct answer.

   a. sommersault

   b. summersault

   c. somersault

   d. sumersault

6. What is the plural of 'sheep'? _____

7. What is the plural of 'tomato'? _____

8. The following passage contains some spelling mistakes.
Rewrite the passage using the correct spellings.

We'd traveled many miles on the train by the time I woke up. I tried to see through the steemed up window but it was pich black outside. How long before we reeched our destinashun? I had no idea. I only new the duke was waiting and we couldn't be late.

_____

_____

_____

_____

_____

9. Which of the following words is spelt incorrectly?
Circle the letter that corresponds to the correct answer.

a. elegent

b. allege

c. swede

d. enjoyable

10. Jane couldn't enter the race at 9am as it was convenient for her.

Rewrite the above sentence using the correct prefix for 'convenient'.

_____

_____

11. What is the singular of 'geese'? _____

12. "I love the Star Wars films." he said.

Rewrite the above sentence as reported speech.

_____

End of Test 1

Test 2

You have **10** minutes to complete this test

1. Which of the following punctuation marks can be used to separate two closely linked sentences? Circle the correct letter.

a. colon

b. comma

c. semi-colon

d. question mark

2. They argued over a simple understanding, she didn't know why.

Rewrite the above sentence using the correct prefix for 'understanding'.

_____

_____

3. What is the plural of 'octopus'? _____

4. The following passage contains some punctuation mistakes.
Rewrite the passage using the correct punctuation.

Edward; who had been working at the bakery for many years led the customers in through the door He hesitated when he saw Mary. It's fine, we're open." Mary said

_____

_____

_____

_____

5. Which of the following sentences uses colons correctly?
Circle the letter that corresponds to the correct answer.

a. We had: seen him on Wednesday after playing football.

b. They'd love to: move house, it's just too expensive.

c. Only three people remained: Jack, Sue and Tony.

d. You can only come: on Monday.

6. What is the singular of 'millenia' _____

The following passage contains grammatical errors. Each numbered line contains either one mistake or no mistakes. Circle the mistakes that you can find.

7. We reached the classroom, Tom and Emma was dancing in the middle of

8. the room. Steven was arguing with Toby. Suddenly the lights went out

9. and an scream was heard. I wanted to run, but my legs had turned to jelly.

10. "What should we do." I whispered. "I have no idea." Oliver replied.

11. "I worked in a bank for three years." said Michael.

    Rewrite the above sentence as reported speech.

    _____

12. If he had seen the film, James may have recognised the actor.

    What type of word is 'may' in the sentence above?
    Circle the letter that corresponds to the correct answer.

a. preposition

b. modal verb

c. adverbial

d. adverb

End of Test 2

Test 3

You have **10** minutes to complete this test

The following passage contains spelling mistakes. Each numbered line contains either one mistake or no mistakes. Circle the words that contain spelling mistakes.

1. Dr Jekyll is a good and clever doctor, but he has a bad part in his caracter that

2. no one but himself nows about. In his studies he discovers a drug which enables

3. him to seperate this bad part from the good and to make that part into a real

4. person—Mr Hyde. By taking his drug, Dr Jekyll can turn into Mr Hyde and enjoy being

5. evil without any twinges of consience. Dr Jekyll then discovers that he changes into

6. Mr Hyde without intending to do so. This has dire concequences.

7. What is the plural of 'box'? _____

8. The following passage contains some spelling mistakes.
Rewrite the passage using the correct spellings.

The Southern Upland Way is a long-distance path that's been designatted as one of 'Scotland's Great Trails', and it is the longest in the currant group of 29 trails. It is perhaps less well-nown than many of the United Kingdom's other long-distance trails, and when you start looking into what it actually offers for walkers this becomes quite suprising. For example, the Southern Upland Way was Britain's first offishal coast-to-coast route.

9. For each line of the following passage circle the correctly spelt word that completes the passage in correct English.

a. The dainty, sparkling white **knoding   knodding   nodding   noding** heads of

b. snowdrops with their **jewel   juwel   juewel   juwle** -green centres appear in

c. the coldest of **wether   whether   weather   wheather** conditions. They are

d. one of the first bulbs to appear and **signafy   signiphy   cignify   signify** that

e. spring is on its way. Snowdrops can **briten   brightten   britten   brighten** up

f. your garden whilst other plants are **dorment   doormant   dormant doorment**.

10. Which of the following am I least likely to do on Tuesday?
Circle the letter next to the correct answer.

a. I will probably run a mile on Tuesday.

b. I shan't go for a walk on Tuesday.

c. I could bake a cake on Tuesday.

d. I might tidy my room on Tuesday.

End of Test 3

Test 4

You have **10** minutes to complete this test

1. Circle the adverbial in the following sentence.

Sally always stops and chats with her neighbours.

2. The following passage contains grammatical errors. Each line contains either one error or no errors. Circle the errors that you can find.

a. When people are bought before a court of law, either because they are

b. charged with an crime or because they are involved in a private quarrel that has

c. been brought to court, the court has: two main duties to carry out before it

d. decides the matter.

3. Which of the following sentences uses the present progressive form? Circle the correct corresponding letter.

a. Caroline is working over the weekend.

b. James was not going to the party.

c. Norman wants to book a table at the restaurant.

d. The couple were waiting patiently in the queue.

4. Add words before and after the word 'puppy' to form your own noun phrase.

_____

5. Leonardo Da Vinci painted the Mona Lisa.

Rewrite the above sentence in the passive voice.

_____

_____

6. Add the missing commas to the following sentences.

a. For supper last night I had chicken rice peas and carrots.

b. Tony's favourite bands were Passenger The 1975 The Beatles and Metallica.

c. Sarah's friends were Jon who loved dancing Mary and Colin.

d. Navigating through snow sleet wind and darkness is difficult.

9. Which of the following words is spelt incorrectly? Circle the correct answer.

a. irate

b. maim

c. tenden

d. whine

In the following passage you have been given a choice of words.
Circle the word that makes the most sense in correct English.

10. Nowadays laurel bushes **is are were was** often grown for ornamental

11. purposes in people's gardens, but in **past before ancient future**

12. Greece and Rome poets **which were when would** crowned with

13. wreaths made **at in of have** laurel.

End of Test 4

Test 5

You have 10 minutes to complete this test

1. Can you rewrite the following sentence using the correct punctuation.

"Do you really want sausages for your tea, mum asked, "You had them on Monday Tuesday Wednesday and Thursday!

_____

_____

_____

2. Which of the following words is spelt correctly? Circle the correct answer.

a. caurtious

b. courteous

c. concience

d. concequence

3. Emma was sad, as she had sufficient funds in her account to pay her bills.
Rewrite the above sentence using the correct prefix for 'sufficient'.

_____

_____

4. The following passage contains some spelling mistakes.
Rewrite the passage with the spelling mistakes corrected.

Sientists on Earth stay in touch with spacecraft threw networks of antenna positioned arownd the planet. The USA have satelite dishes at three sites: in Australea, Spain and the USA.

_____

_____

_____

_____

5. In the following passage you have been given a choice of words.
Circle the word that makes the most sense in correct English.

If you're thinking about **an of a two** night out camping with a friend

those though then this a two-person tent is definitely the way to go.

Carrying **this those your mine** gear becomes so much easier without

two tents **too two to the** lug about.

End of Test 5

Test 6

You have **10** minutes to complete this test

1. Geoffs cooking skills, if you can call them skills, left a lot to be desired.

What is wrong with the above sentence? Circle the letter that corresponds to the error.

a. There are too many commas.

b. 'Geoffs' needs an apostrophe before the 's'.

c. A colon is missing.

d. 'Geoffs' needs an apostrophe after the 's'.

2. Rewrite the following sentence adding the missing capital letters and punctuation.

i cant see the birds from down here cried tom i need to stand back a bit

_____

_____

3. "Help" screamed Toby as he fell from the ladder!

Rewrite the above sentence correcting any punctuation errors.

_____

_____

4. Which of the following sentences uses commas correctly?
Circle the letter that corresponds to the correct sentence.

a. My friend Vijay, is a wonderful dancer.

b. Jackie will wear a black jacket, and red trousers.

c. We were out of milk, I went to the store.

d. After the show, James will be signing autographs.

5. What is the plural of 'diagnosis' _____

6. Which of the following sentences uses apostrophes correctly?
Circle the letter that corresponds to the correct answer.

a. I'm going to the zoo: it's the zookeeper's day off.

b. Julies' idea wasn't accepted.

c. The companys' management won't take responsibility.

d. We invited the children's parent's to the recital.

In the following passage you have been given a choice of words.
Circle the word that makes the most sense in correct English.

7. Your body   tries **uses** has is   different fuels for energy depending on the

8. intensity of the exercises. It is therefore important   this those **that** the   your

9. body has enough energy. Good nutrition   was where will **is**   vital to

10. ensure that   this that your **you**   body's needs are met. Eating carbohydrates

11. is   **a** an of in   good way to get energy. The right types of carbohydrates,

12. such as oats,   could shall which **can**   release energy to your body slowly.

13. However, other types   in at **of** which   carbohydrates provide your body

14. **which** when were with   quick, instant energy—such as sugar.

End of Test 6

Test 7

You have 10 minutes to complete this test

1. Which of the following words is not an adverb?
   Circle the letter that corresponds to the correct answer.

   a. maybe

   b. rapidly

   c. north

   d. terrible

2. She put two bowls of milk on the floor for the cats.

   Write down the determiner or determiners from the above sentence.

   _____

3. That book is mine.

   In the above sentence is 'that' a determiner or a pronoun? Circle the correct answer.

   a. determiner

   b. pronoun

4. Which of the following sentences does not contain a conjunction?
Circle the letter that corresponds to the correct answer.

a. I like eating but I don't like washing up afterwards.

b. The students were unhappy with their teacher; he wasted time.

c. I love bananas but dislike apples, pears and oranges.

d. Oliver can stay out until the clock strikes twelve.

5. What is the plural of 'half'? _____

6. The money was counted by the cashier.

Rewrite the above sentence in the active voice. Discard any unnecessary words.

_____

The following passage contains punctuation errors. But can you find them?
Each numbered line has one mistake. Circle each punctuation error.

7. Josie remembered when shopping was very different. Shed enjoy a special trip,

8. on Wednesday's, to the fishmongers. All the different types of fish would be

9. lined up. There was plaice, mackeral cod, haddock and little sardines. She

10. took ages to choose All that choice! Eventually she would choose cod though.

11. The fishmonger wou'd smile; he knew Josie always chose cod.

12. John Harrison, who is 68, has just retired.

Which word in the above sentence is a relative pronoun?

_____

13. Which of the following sentences is written in the passive voice?
Circle the corresponding correct letter.

a. James devoured his icecream; chocolate was his favourite flavour.

b. The dogs were fed twice a day by Maisie and Jenny.

c. Jake kicked the football and scored a goal.

d. Doris ate her sandwich quickly: she was starving!

14. Which of the following words is spelt correctly?
Circle the correct corresponding letter.

a. flurish

b. merchent

c. resite

d. tyrant

End of Test 7

Test 8

You have **10** minutes to complete this test

The following passage contains spelling errors. Can you find them?
Each numbered line has either one mistake or no mistake. Circle each spelling error.

1. It was getting late when Toby and Ben realised that they where lost. The

2. church was in sight and there, beside it, the cemetary. A cold shiver went

3. down Toby's spine, but he was too embarrased to let Ben know that he

4. was scared. They trudged on, each trying to recognise where they were.

5. Knowing they weren't equiped to spend the night outdoors gave them

6. both the impitus to carry on, but neither boy had brought food or water

7. and they knew their clothes wouldn't be suficiently warm for much longer.

8. Which of the following sentences uses commas correctly?
   Circle the letter that corresponds to the correct answer.

a. Once, Michael had been to the doctors he headed back home.

b. The car, that hit the wall was old.

c. Flying back from Sweden, we saw a beautiful sunset.

d. Madge loves to travel, she visits France once a year.

9. Jim usually gets on with everybody he is an understanding person.

The above sentence is missing a semicolon.
Rewrite the sentence adding the missing punctuation mark.

_____

The following passage contains punctuation errors. Each line contains one mistake. Circle the errors in each line.

10. Under the clock he stood and waited. Janice had promised to meet him at 9.40pm,

11. but it was already 9.55pm. Where was she. She was never late. He looked

12. up and down the road; Janice was nowhere to be seen The clock started to chime

13. just as his phone rang. "Is that you Janice"? he asked, but the caller hung up.

14. He redialed the number, but there was no answer. He looked down, at his watch

15. again. It was now 10.20pm; he would call Janices' phone. But as he started dialling

16. she came running down the street

17. What is the plural of 'elf' _____

18. What is the singular of 'hooves' _____

End of Test 8

Test 9

You have 10 minutes to complete this test

1. After she picks me up, mum is taking me to buy shoes.

Which part of the above sentence is the subordinate clause? Circle the correct answer.

a. After she picks me up

b. mum is taking

c. mum is taking me to buy shoes

d. to buy shoes

2. My brother, Michael, is six years old.

Write down the nouns that appear in the above sentence.

_____

3. Circle the part of the following sentence that contains a grammatical error.

I would of come home at seven, but I didn't know the time.

4. Rewrite the sentence from question 3 above without the grammatical error.

_____

_____

Circle the correct word from each line of the following passage so that the passage makes sense in standard English.

5. Just before breakfast, I put some bird seed **under at on in** the path near the

6. bird table. I checked **those they then that** there was some bacon rind

7. dangling on the string **with from that those** a branch of the apple tree and

8. that there **was were where is** still some peanuts in the container.

9. Write down the pronoun from the following sentence.

   David bought himself some crisps.

   _____

10. Turn left at the crossroads into Station Road.

    What type of word is 'left' in the sentence above.
    Circle the letter that corresponds to the correct answer.

a. conjunction

b. adverb

c. noun

d. adjective

29

11. I got 50p change from the one pound coin I gave the shopkeeper.

Write down any determiners from the above sentence.

_____

12. I won't stand by the woman who smells of strawberries.

Write down the relative clause in the above sentence.

_____

13. The author was uninspirred and worried about his imminant deadline.

Draw a circle around any misspelt words in the above sentence.

14. Can you rewrite the misspelt word or words from question 13 spelt correctly?

_____

End of Test 9

Test 10

You have 10 minutes to complete this test

The following passage contains spelling errors. Can you find them?
Each numbered line has either one mistake or no mistake. Circle each spelling error.

1. Their are at least 100 billion galaxies in the Universe. Some are enormous,

2. containing hundreds of billions of stars. Others are much smaller, sometimes

3. containing fuwer than a million stars. There are many more small galaxies than

4. giant galaxies, even though the dwarf galaxies tend to be swalowed by their

5. larger naybours over time. Some galaxies are very large, yet contain very few

6. stars. These feint galaxies are made almost entirely of gas, so in photographs

7. they appear as a smudge in the sky. We live in a galaxy of about 100 billion stars

8. called the Milky Whey.

9. Which of the following words is spelt incorrectly?
   Circle the correct corresponding letter.

a. rural

b. mere

c. ernest

d. procure

10. He ate his breakfast before the sun came up.

Rewrite the above sentence so that the adverbial becomes a fronted adverbial.

_____

_____

11. My dog barked loudly whenever the doorbell rang.

In the above sentence what sort of word is 'whenever'?
Circle the letter that corresponds to the correct answer.

a. co-ordinating conjunction

b. verb

c. adverb

d. subordinating conjunction

12. Write a sentence in the passive voice using the following words:

was   dog   squirrel   the   by   chased   the

_____

_____

13. Write a sentence in the active voice using the following words:

    are   film   watch   going   we   tonight   to   a

    _____

    _____

Test 11

You have **10** minutes to complete this test

1. The following passage contains punctuation errors.
Rewrite the passage using the correct punctuation.

"My heart leaps up when I behold a rainbow in the sky." wrote William wordsworth, the famous poet and most of us share his feelings when we are lucky enough to see a rainbow. there's an old saying that theres a pot of gold at the end of a rainbow, but have you ever tried to reach a rainbow's end. Of course it's impossible, because a rainbow is just the result of raindrops refracting and reflecting light from our Sun

2. Underline the prepositions in the following sentences.

a. Hugh kicked the ball <u>across</u> the field.

b. Her violin case was placed <u>under</u> the desk.

c. Emma really wanted to sit <u>beside</u> her friend Stella.

d. Jack and Maria went <u>through</u> the door separately.

e. <u>Underneath</u> the water lurked the infamous monster.

Test 12

You have **10** minutes to complete this test

1. Write five words that end in 'ough'. Each word must pronounce the 'ough' differently.

_____   _____

_____   _____

_____

2. Write the following words in the correct columns.
Some words may appear in more than one column.

under, slowly, elephant, young, anger, rapidly, always, Sunday, enormous

Nouns	Adverbs	Prepositions	Adjectives
_____	_____	_____	_____
_____	_____	_____	_____
_____	_____	_____	_____
_____	_____	_____	_____
_____	_____	_____	_____

3. Which of the following words is spelt correctly?
   Circle the correct corresponding letter.

a. commited

b. errant

c. endevour

d. delibarate

4. Give the plural forms of these words.

a. echo   _____

b. gateau   _____

c. louse   _____

d. vertebra   _____

5. Which of the following words is spelt incorrectly? Circle the correct corresponding letter.

a. exhilaration

b. acquire

c. sober

d. temparate

End of Test 12

Test 13

You have **10** minutes to complete this test

1. Underline the prepositions in the following sentences.

a. Peter preferred to read in the library.

b. Take your sister with you.

c. You need to go down the stairs and through the door.

d. Please sign your name on the dotted line after you've read the script.

e. Mary swam across the swimming pool.

2. Which of the following sentences is punctuated properly?
Circle the letter that corresponds to the correct answer.

a. Jane's hung her mums washing on Mrs Brass's washing line.

b. Jane's hung her mums' washing on Mrs Bras's washing line.

c. Janes' hung her mums' washing on Mrs Brass's washing line.

d. Jane's hung her mum's washing on Mrs Brass's washing line.

3. What tenses are the following sentences written in?

a. Carla laughed at the monkey. _____

b. They will meet at the library. _____

c. Tom stumbled off of the ladder. _____

d. Sue is running for the bus. _____

e. I am eating my supper. _____

f. Dogs often chase cats. _____

The following passage contains punctuation errors. Each numbered line contains either one mistake or no mistake. Circle the errors that you can find.

4. Lord Mortans lights were still on. His heavy curtains were blue and green, just like the

5. sea. A lantern, hanging by the door threw a pool of soft light over the drive. Finlay

6. stared and stared, as if he had never seen bright light before. In the dark of the night,

7. nothing had looked quite right and many things looked really frightening, the spooky

8. branches of the trees, the fallen log, the movement of moonlight. But now, in the clear

9. light, finlay could see there was nothing ghostly about the house at all.

End of Test 13

Test 14

You have 10 minutes to complete this test

1. Rewrite the following misspelt words correctly.

   a. seldum _____

   b. imminant _____

   c. deliberet _____

   d. obay _____

   e. comrad _____

   f. forcast _____

   g. vegtable _____

2. Circle the correct verb form for each of these sentences.

   a. Michael and Emma (was / were) looking forward to Christmas.

   b. Peter jumped out of bed and (throw / threw) back the curtains.

   c. They (are / is) unable to go to the party.

   d. Kate (eat / ate) her dinner quickly.

   e. Simon (drink / drank) the whole carton of orange juice.

3. The following passage contains spelling mistakes. Rewrite the passage using the correct spellings.

Amung the birds of prey are the buzzards, which are rarther like eagles but smaller and less powerful. The buzzard is larger than the partrige. They are found all over the world exept in the Australian region. Only the common buzzard lives and nests in Great Britain. It is a hansome bird, dark brown above and usually barred brown and white below, with brite yellow legs and yellow on its curved bill. It has a week mewing cry and a fine soring flight.

4. What is the singular of 'wives' _____

End of Test 14

Test 15

You have 10 minutes to complete this test

The following passage contains punctuation errors. Each numbered line contains either one mistake or no mistakes. Underline the errors that you can find.

1. "It's a beautiful morning for a run" said Ally. "I'm too tired." replied Tom. "Oh come on

2. lazybones!" laughed Ally. Theyd started running together three weeks previously.

3. Tom was the slower of the two, but Ally always waited for him to catch up. The runs

4. were wonderful. sometimes they would run across the fields and see all sorts of

5. wildlife: buzzards, herons, kingfishers, and even stoats. They both came home glad

6. they'd gone, even if Tom was less than enthusiastic beforehand! It had started

7. because Ally wanted to run a marathon. When Allys application form had arrived Tom

8. had seen it and decided to run to. They'd started their training in October, but the

9. marathon was only weeks away now and neither was sure theyd be ready in time.

10. Only one of the following sentences is punctuated correctly.
Circle the letter that corresponds to the correct one.

a. I always meet Joseph on a wednesday afternoon.

b. We can go for a bike ride on Friday (if it's not raining.)

c. Nadia's mother loved to dance, especially on Fridays.

d. The bearded man, Dave Crom stores bacon in his trousers.

11. I went to school with Tim Sue and Craig went elsewhere.

Rewrite the above sentence adding a comma so that it is clear that I only went to school with Tim.

_____

_____

12. Which of the following sentences uses apostrophes correctly?
Circle the letter that corresponds to the correct answer.

a. Mary's father worked at the factory. His shifts were awful.

b. Jon's book's fell on the ground.

c. Kate and Bellas' family's always travelled together.

d. Cora's cat walked all over Ben's brothers coat.

13. Rewrite the following sentence, inserting a semicolon so that it is punctuated correctly.

Ally and Tom are training for a marathon they run together every other day.

_____

_____

14. Louise was nervous and she wouldn't be able to relax until after the exam.

Which word from the above sentence is a subordinating conjunction?
Circle the letter that corresponds to the correct word.

a. and

b. able

c. until

d. after

End of Test 15

Test 16

You have **10** minutes to complete this test

1. Complete each of the following sentences as a metaphor.

a. The calm lake was a _____

b. Her tears were a _____

c. The crocodile's teeth were white _____

d. The stormy ocean was a _____

e. The field was a _____

2. Write four words that begin with a hyphenated prefix.

a. _____

b. _____

c. _____

d. _____

3. Fill in the blank spaces with the correct word using either 'to', 'two' or 'too'.

a. "I'm _____ tired _____ walk home." the boy said.

b. _____ girls travelled _____ the party.

c. James went _____ the shop _____ buy some milk.

d. It was _____ far _____ drive for just _____ days.

4. Which of the following words is spelt correctly?
Circle the letter that corresponds to the correct answer.

a. pronounciation

b. resturant

c. suficient

d. persuade

End of Test 16

Test 17

You have **10** minutes to complete this test

1. Sentances should reflect the severety of the crime.

Rewrite the above sentence correcting any misspelt words.

_____

_____

2. The following passage contains punctuation errors.
Rewrite the passage using the correct punctuation.

"Youll never guess what I've just seen said Thomas, excitedly.
"What's that" asked Henrietta
"Toby's mums got a broomstick in the boot of her car. maybe she's a witch!
"Don't be ridiculous! we're all going out for halloween tonight" replied Henrietta.
"Oh yeah, I'd forgotten about that." said thomas

_____

_____

_____

_____

_____

_____

3. Which of the following sentences is punctuated correctly?
Circle the letter that corresponds to the correct answer.

a. Charlie works three days a week, Wednesdays, Fridays and Saturdays.

b. "I told you not to feed the dog"!

c. Sally likes bacon sandwiches: Molly prefers tuna sandwiches.

d. The weather, I was happy to see, was beginning to clear.

4. Which of the following words is spelt correctly.
Circle the letter that corresponds to the correct answer.

a. tipewriter

b. restrane

c. primative

d. veil

End of Test 17

Test 18

You have 10 minutes to complete this test

1. Write the following words in reverse alphabetical order.

resign   reserve   reverse   revive   repent   revoke

a. _____   b. _____

c. _____   d. _____

e. _____   f. _____

2. Circle the modal verb in the following sentence.

I must stop eating biscuits if I'm to lose weight!

3. Which of the following sentences does not indicate certainty? Circle the letter that corresponds to the correct answer.

a. Sonya works on Mondays so can't travel on that day.

b. "Just come to the class, I'll pay for you!"

c. "I might make a fish pie for tea." said mum.

d. William couldn't understand what the German man said.

4. Which of the following sentences uses the past perfect form?

a. Craig drove all night to get to the hospital on time.

b. "What time did you arrive?" asked Anne.

c. By lunchtime, I had walked four miles.

d. The price of bananas went up last week.

5. I pulled a muscle in my back as I was putting my socks on.

Write down the subordinate clause from the sentence above.

_____

_____

End of Test 18

Test 19

You have 10 minutes to complete this test

1. He knew what his superpower would be the ability to become invisible.

   Rewrite the above sentence adding a colon so that it is punctuated correctly.

   _____

   _____

2. The following passage contains punctuation errors.
   Rewrite the passage so that it is written correctly.

   Meddling meredith is angry and confused by claims that she is not cooperating with the FBI in its investigation into espionage a senior US prosecutor complained on monday that investigators working on the case were unable to contact Meredith at her home address

   _____

   _____

   _____

   _____

   _____

   _____

3. Which of the following sentences uses the subjunctive form?
Circle the correct answer.

a. It is vital that Elizabeth eats everyday.

b. If he trained to be a magician, he could make us disappear.

c. I wish that I were able to fly.

d. In two weeks, I shall be able to hold my breath for longer than one minute.

4. The library often holds meetings downstairs.

Which word in the above sentence is an adverb?

_____

5. Match each of the following words with their word class. Use each word only once.

    set   unless   loudly   they   huge   hold   courage

a. adjective   _____

b. abstract noun   _____

c. adverb   _____

d. pronoun   _____

e. conjunction   _____

f. collective noun   _____

g. verb   _____

End of Test 19

Test 20

You have 10 minutes to complete this test

1. The following passage contains spelling mistakes.
   Rewrite the passage using the correct spellings.

   A large persentage of the eggs sold in Britain are battry-produced. However, if you're lucky enough to live near to an old-fashoned farm, where the hens are free to rome about, you can probly get well-flavored eggs with rich-coloured yokes.

   _____

   _____

   _____

   _____

   _____

2. David had to **simple** the directions so that they were easier to follow.

   Rewrite the above sentence, adding the correct suffix to the word 'simple'.

   _____

3. Write the plural of 'eyelash'.   _____

4. Write an antonym for each of the following words by adding a prefix.

a. agree _____

b. forgiving _____

c. excusable _____

d. lead _____

e. tolerant _____

f. entity _____

5. Punctuate the following sentence correctly.

i will always love you swooned isabella always

_____

6. Complete each of the following sentences as metaphors.

a. The sun _____

b. The falling snowflakes _____

c. Tobias is _____

d. Her long hair _____

End of Test 20

Test 21

You have **10** minutes to complete this test

1. Shirley whispered that she had exciting news.

Rewrite the above sentence as direct speech.

_____

2. The following passage contains spelling mistakes.
Rewrite the passage using the correct spellings.

Kathleen was desparate to acheive a trophy for her sculpture, but there was no garantee that she woud. In her experiance the sculptors that produced the largest peices usually gained the neccessary points for a trophy. But she held out hope for this year's anual competition; she really didn't want to loose again.

_____

_____

_____

_____

_____

3. "The biscuit's are for Wendys mums dog—you mustn't eat them!

Rewrite the above sentence with the correct punctuation.

_____

_____

4. The invitation stated, "You are **cordial** invited to the party."

Rewrite the sentence above adding the correct suffix to 'cordial'.

_____

_____

5. Which of the following sentences uses hyphens correctly.
Circle the letter that corresponds to the correct answer.

a. He bought a very-elegant, state-of-the-art, apartment.

b. He bought-a very elegant, state of the art, apartment.

c. He bought a very elegant, state-of-the-art, apartment.

d. He bought-a very elegant, state of the art, apartment.

End of Test 21

Test 22

You have 10 minutes to complete this test

1. There's never been a better time to buy.

   Why is there an apostrophe in 'there's'?
   Circle the letter that corresponds to the correct answer.

a. It shows possession.

b. It makes it easier to say.

c. It is a contraction of 'there' and 'has'.

d. It is a contraction of 'there' and 'is'.

2. Complete the following sentence using suitable possessive pronouns.

   The biscuits I found in the cupboard were _____ . Jake

   thought they were _____ , but I knew _____

   were chocolate chip.

3. List the determiners in the following sentence.

   Lisa put some rice and an egg on to cook whilst she did her homework.

   _____

4. Write the contracted forms of the following words.

a. shall not _____

b. would not _____

c. I had _____

d. did not _____

e. they would _____

5. Change the sentence below into a list using bullet points.

To make delicious muffins you need: flour, two eggs, butter, sugar, vanilla extract and blueberries.

_____

_____

_____

_____

_____

_____

6. Jack Taylor last year's winner is trailing by two points.

Place commas into the above sentence to show parenthesis.

7. Write a synonym for each of the following words.

a. alter _____

b. create _____

c. burrow _____

d. novice _____

Test 23

You have **10** minutes to complete this test

1. A smart, professional businessman in a grey suit entered the office.

   Write down the longest noun phrase from the sentence above.

   _____

2. Carlton, who scored the winning goal, was congratulated by his team.

   Write down the relative clause from the above sentence.

   _____

3. He's on the phone at the moment.

   Write down the preposition in the above sentence.

   _____

4. The following passage contains some spelling mistakes.
Rewrite the passage using the correctly spelt word.

It was a credit to the staff that the students had low levels of anxciety in the lead-up to the tests. The importance of preparation had been instilled in the children as its positive affect cannot be exagerated. After an exhorstive search on the internet for a venue for the exams, a siutable location was found. Afterwards, the staff were justafiably proud of the children's achievements.

Test 24

You have **10** minutes to complete this test

1. Kevin bought eight charming Victorian silver ornaments at the market.

   List the adjectives that appear in the above sentence.

   _____

2. Is the following sentence written in the active voice or the passive voice?

   The boys were chased by a tiny barking dog.

   _____

3. Circle the letter that corresponds to the sentence that uses tenses incorrectly.

   a. I will read as much as I could this year.

   b. Maisie had been cooking for a year before her sister learned to cook.

   c. I must go to the bakers, or I will run out of bread.

   d. If horses were carnivorous they could eat meat.

4. For each line of the following passage, circle the correctly spelt word to complete the sentence in correct English.

a. He knew it was a **conspirracy   conspirasy   connspiracy   conspiracy**

b. against him. It was a **sobarring   sobbaring   sobering   soberring** thought

c. to think that he was now **purseeved   perseved   perceived   percieved** to be

d. the underdog in all of this. His friends had become his **fose   foes   foze   foez**,

e. and now they were **shuning   shunning   shunnen   shunen** him.

5. Which of the following sentences does not use the progressive form?
Circle the letter that corresponds to the correct answer.

a. Clarissa was going to put ten candles on the cake.

b. Duncan and Leslie are sharing the tent.

c. Finlay wants to eat the whole pie.

d. Yvonne is creating an eiderdown for her grandmother.

6. Geoff's hat is certainly large but, in my opinion, mine is even bigger.

Which word in the above sentence is a pronoun? Circle the letter that corresponds to the correct answer.

a. mine

b. large

c. hat

d. bigger

7. Rewrite the following sentences using Standard English.

a. "You must of seen it!" exclaimed Mark, "It was enormous!"

_____

_____

b. They ain't getting nothing until Wednesday.

_____

_____

c. We was really late for school and my teacher weren't happy.

_____

End of Test 24

Test 25

You have **10** minutes to complete this test

1. Give an antonym for the word 'abundance'. _____

2. Put these words into alphabetical order.

prosperous   pretext   promotion   premonition   promontory   prominent

a. _____   b. _____

c. _____   d. _____

e. _____   f. _____

3. Write a one-word synonym for the words in bold.

a. Diane **made up her mind** to catch the 7.45pm train.

_____

b. The whole family liked to go to the theatre **once a year**.

_____

c. Joe had to **put off** posting the letter, as he didn't have a stamp.

_____

4. Add a conjunction to the following sentences using a different word for each answer.

a. I drank a glass of water _____ I was thirsty.

b. Marcel can stay until 3pm _____ he's not due home until later.

c. Dominic waited at the station _____ Oliver arrived.

5. Create a noun ending in 'ion' from the given verbs.

a. eject _____

b. dilate _____

c. adapt _____

d. fixate _____

6. Which of the following words is spelt correctly.
Circle the letter that corresponds to the correct answer.

a. inordible

b. plenteful

c. miserly

d. pospone

End of Test 25

Test 26

You have 10 minutes to complete this test

1. Write two definitions for the following words.

   Stagger

   a. _____

   b. _____

   Enterprise

   a. _____

   b. _____

2. Rewrite the following sentences using the correct punctuation.

   a. jason whispered im coming now

   _____

   b. are we there yet the children whined

   _____

   c. its time you were both in bed said Sarah the babysitter

   _____

   _____

d. at university jane specialised in three subjects latin german and french

3. The following passage contains spelling mistakes. Rewrite the passage with the misspelt words spelt correctly.

Winter heliotrope produces its clusters of vanila-scented, pale perple flowers from January to April. A valuble early nectar sauce for pollinating insects, the blooms are folowed by a carpit of kidney-shaped leaves.

4. What is the plural of 'quiz'

5. What is the singular of 'species'

End of Test 26

Test 27

You have 10 minutes to complete this test

1. Rewrite the following passage using correct punctuation and starting a new line each time a new person starts to speak.

where are you going on holiday this year enquired susan to india replied cora i havent been there and id love to go exclaimed susan you should cora laughed

_____

_____

_____

_____

_____

In the following passage circle a word in each line so that the passage makes sense and is spelt correctly.

2. The farm was **cited   sighted   sited   sitted** down in the valley. They used to

3. keep cattle but now it was only a **poultry   pawltry   pultry   poltry** farm, with over

4. 350 chickens. Farming was **tyring   tyering   tiring   tiering** work and everyone

5. **leand   lent   loaned   lend** a hand. Even eight-year-old Jack!

71

6. The following passage contains spelling mistakes.
Rewrite the passage correcting any misspelt words.

Annabel sailed out of the harbor, abord the yocht. Today she would be sailing entyrely alone, and she was tremendusly excited. The hole fleat had sailed together on Wensday, but today she had the sea to herself. She siezed the helm and steered the boat to the left as she susspected the wind would be in her favor if she went in that direction.

End of Test 27

Test 28

You have **10** minutes to complete this test

1. For each of the following words add the 'ous' suffix. Rewrite the new word.

a. miscellany _____

b. harmony _____

c. envy _____

d. infect _____

e. courage _____

f. fibre _____

2. Which of the following words is spelt incorrectly?
Circle the letter that corresponds to the correct answer.

a. stoop

b. impudent

c. famin

d. liable

3. What is the plural of 'torpedo'? _____

4. Rewrite the following passage using the correct words, from those in bold, to complete each sentence so that the passage makes sense.

Cheshire is **an a some other** English county with a short coastline on the Irish Sea. It **was by is has** bordered by seven other counties. The River Mersey forms the northern boundary **was when with were** Lancashire, and the county touches the corner **at by over of** Yorkshire in the northeast. Shropshire is the boundary **at on before after** the south.

End of Test 28

Test 29

You have 10 minutes to complete this test

1. The students measured the volume of the chemicals accurately.

   What type of word is 'accurately' in the sentence above? Circle the correct letter.

   a. preposition

   b. modal verb

   c. adverbial

   d. adverb

2. My French teacher, who came to England in 1990, loves spinach.

   In the above sentence what is 'who came to England in 1990' an example of?

   a. relative clause

   b. noun phrase

   c. adverbial

   d. main clause

3. Write whether the following sentences are active or passive.

a. Jake was eating a pear. _____

b. The picture was painted by Sarah. _____

c. Sue opened the present. _____

d. James kicked the ball with his foot. _____

e. The spoon was left on the table by Kate. _____

The following passage contains spelling mistakes, but not on every line.
Can you spot them? Circle the words that are misspelt.

4. The situation was extremely aukward. John and Caroline thought that the flat

5. would be able to accomodate their whole family, but it would seem that it was

6. too small. The children would have to share the single bedroom and John

7. would have to sleep in the attatched nursery. The situation was very familiar,

8. this had happened before. They had not had suficient space in their first flat

9. and this move was supposed to solve that problem. Acording to the details

10. their should have been three bedrooms, but it was now apparent that there were

11. only two. They would have to resine themselves to continuing their search.

End of Test 29

Test 30

You have 10 minutes to complete this test

1. Which of the following words is spelt incorrectly?
   Circle the correct corresponding letter.

a. resign

b. prosperous

c. percieve

d. prominent

2. Write a sentence using a noun, an adjective and the verb 'burst'.

   _____

3. Which of the following words is spelt correctly?
   Circle the correct answer.

a. abundent

b. incesant

c. sordid

d. goverment

4. The glistening snow covered the field.

   Write down the noun phrase from the above sentence.

   _____

5. Rewrite the following sentence replacing 'Mr and Mrs Brown's' with a suitable pronoun.

   I'd love to see Mr and Mrs Brown's new house.

   _____

   _____

6. What is the plural of 'kangaroo'?   _____

7. Use one word from each of the columns to create six new compound words.

cent	hold
just	ridge
cart	page
up	in
ram	ice
cab	rally

   _____   _____   _____

   _____   _____   _____

End of Test 30

Test 31

You have 10 minutes to complete this test

1. What is the plural of 'crisis'? _____

2. Sanjay was taught to cook by an Italian lady.

    Rewrite the above sentence using the active voice.

    _____

    _____

3. Write the root word for each of the following.

    a. abnormal   b. immature

    c. misbehave   d. happier

    e. bilingual   f. collapsible

4. Write a recognised abbreviation for each of the following.

a. World wildlife fund _____

b. New Zealand _____

c. Post office _____

d. Megabyte _____

e. Personal computer _____

5. Which of the following sentences is punctuated correctly? Circle the letter that corresponds to the correct answer.

a. Lets eat granny

b. Lets eat granny,

c. Let's eat, granny.

d. Let's eat granny

Test 32

You have **10** minutes to complete this test

1. Rewrite the following extract so that it is punctuated correctly.

We are looking for volunteers from the community to join us in enhancing the opportunities and experiences of Valley Park Primary Schools children. There are various ways in which you could help as a paired teacher as a sports coach or referee as a chaperone on outings or by sharing a specialist knowledge you have. The paired reading scheme operates every morning from 9.00 - 9.30am. helpers elect to come as many mornings as they feel able and full training is given. Pupils responses have been wholly positive one pupil recently said, "I thought I'd never be able to read. But thanks to Mr Po, whos been helping me for three months Ive just read 'Harry Potter and the Philosopher's Stone' all on my own."

_____

_____

_____

_____

_____

_____

_____

_____

2. Use one word from each of the columns to create six new compound words.

      clam   me
      the   he
      he   our
      do   address
      her   ring
      bat   or

_____   _____

_____   _____

_____   _____

End of Test 32

Answers

Test 1.

1. a

2. b

3. c

4. b

5. c

6. sheep

7. tomatoes

8. The misspelt words are shown in bold using their correct spelling.

   We'd **travelled** many miles on the train by the time I woke up. I tried to see through the **steamed** up window but it was **pitch** black outside. How long before we **reached** our **destination**? I had no idea. I only **knew** the duke was waiting and we couldn't be late.

9. a

10. Jane couldn't enter the race at 9am as it was **in**convenient for her.

11. goose

12. He said that he loved the Star Wars films.

Test 2

1. c

2. They argued over a simple **mis**understanding, she didn't know why.

3. octopuses

4. Edward, who had been working at the bakery for many years, led the customers in through the door. He hesitated when he saw Mary. "It's fine, we're open." Mary said.

   comma after 'Edward', comma after 'years', full stop after 'door', speech marks before 'It's', full stop after 'said'

5. c

6. millenium

7. was
   should be 'were'

8. *no mistakes in line 8*

9. an
   should be 'a'

10. ?
    there should be a question mark after 'do' rather than a full stop

11. Michael said he worked in a bank for three years.

12. b

Test 3

1. character
   the letter 'h' is missing

2. knows
   the letter 'k' is missing

3. separate
   replace the second 'e' with 'a'

4. *no mistakes in line 4*

5. conscience
   the letter 'c' is missing

6. consequences
   replace second 'c' with 's'

7. boxes

8. The Southern Upland Way is a long-distance path that's been **designated** as one of 'Scotland's Great Trails', and it is the longest in the **current** group of 29 trails. It is perhaps less **well-known** than many of the United Kingdom's other long-distance trails, and when you start looking into what it actually offers for walkers this becomes quite **surprising**. For example, the Southern Upland Way was Britain's first **official** coast-to-coast route.

   the misspelt words are in bold and have been corrected

9.

a.   nodding

b.   jewel

c.   weather

d.   signify

e.   brighten

f.   dormant

10.   b

Test 4

1.   always

2

a.   bought
should be 'brought'

b.   an
should be 'a'

c.   :
there should not be a colon after 'has'

d.   *there are no mistakes in this line*

3. a

4. The small brown puppy is available for adoption.
there are numerous sentences that can be made, as long as the noun 'puppy' has modifiers (in this case 'The small brown')

5. The Mona Lisa was painted by Leonardo Da Vinci.

6. a. For supper last night I had chicken, rice, peas and carrots.
   b. Tony's favourite bands were Passenger, The 1975, The Beatles and Metallica.
   c. Sarah's friends were Jon, who loved dancing, Mary and Colin.
   d. Navigating through snow, sleet, wind and darkness is difficult.

9. c

10. are

11. ancient

12. were

13. of

Test 5

1. "Do you really want sausages for your tea?" mum asked, "You had them on Monday, Tuesday, Wednesday and Thursday!"

   replace comma after 'tea' with a question mark, add speech marks after the question mark, add a comma after 'Monday' and 'Tuesday', speech marks missing after the exclamation mark at the end of the sentence

2. b

3. Emma was sad, as she had **in**sufficient funds in her account to pay her bills.

4. **Scientists** on Earth stay in touch with spacecraft **through** networks of antenna positioned **around** the planet. The USA have **satellite** dishes at three sites: in **Australia**, Spain and the USA.

5. If you're thinking about **a** night out camping with a friend **then** a two-person tent is definitely the way to go. Carrying **your** gear becomes so much easier without two tents **to** lug about.

Test 6

1. b

2. "I can't see the birds from down here!" cried Tom. "I need to stand back a bit."

3. "Help!" screamed Toby**,** as he fell from the ladder.

   exclamation mark after 'Help', comma after 'Toby', full stop instead of exclamation mark after 'ladder'

4. d
   because the sentence begins with an adverbial

5. diagnoses

6. a

7. Your body **uses** different fuels for energy depending on the

8. intensity of the exercises. It is therefore important **that** your

9. body has enough energy. Good nutrition **is** vital to

10. ensure that **your** body's needs are met. Eating carbohydrates

11. is **a** good way to get energy. The right types of carbohydrates,

12. such as oats, **can** release energy to your body slowly.

13. However, other types **of** carbohydrates provide your body

14. **with** quick, instant energy—such as sugar.

Test 7

1. d

2. two, the

3. a

4. b

5. halves

6. The cashier counted the money.

7. She'd
   missing apostrophe

8. Wednesdays
   'Wednesday's' should not have an apostrophe

9. mackeral, cod
   comma after mackeral

10. *there should be a full stop after 'choose'*

11. would
    replace the apostrophe with the letter 'l'

12. who

13. b

14. d

Test 8

1. were
   instead of 'where'

2. cemetery

3. embarrassed

4. *there are no mistakes in line 4*

5. equipped

6. impetus

7. sufficiently

8. c
   the comma sets off the Introductory Phrase

9. Jim usually gets on with everybody; he is an understanding person.

10. *comma after clock as it is a fronted adverbial*

11. *'?' after 'she' rather than a full stop*

12. *full stop after 'seen'*

13. *?"*
    the question mark should come before the speech marks

14. *the comma after 'down' should be removed*

15. Janice's
    the apostrophe should come after the 'e' in Janice's

16. *there should be a full stop after 'street'*

17. elves

18. hoof

Test 9

1. a
   'After she picks me up' gives additional information about when mum is buying shoes

2. brother, Michael, years

3. of
   should be 'have'

4. I would have come home at seven, but I didn't know the time.

5. on

6. that

7. from

8. were

9. David

10. b

11. the, the

12. who smells of strawberries

13. uninspirred, imminant

14. uninspired, imminent

Test 10

1. Their
   should be 'there'

2. *no mistakes in line 2*

3. fuwer
   should be 'fewer'

4. swalowed
   should be 'swallowed'

5. naybours
   should be 'neighbours'

6. feint
   should be 'faint'

7. *no mistakes in line 7*

8. Whey
   should be 'Way'

9. c

10. Before the sun came up, he ate his breakfast.

11. d

12. The squirrel was chased by the dog.

13. We are going to watch a film tonight.

Test 11

1.
"My heart leaps up when I behold a rainbow in the sky," wrote William **W**ordsworth, the famous poet**,** and most of us share his feelings when we are lucky enough to see a rainbow. **T**here's an old saying that there's a pot of gold at the end of a rainbow, but have you ever tried to reach a rainbow's end**?** Of course it's impossible, because a rainbow is just the result of raindrops refracting and reflecting light from our Sun**.**

line 1. speech marks missing at the beginning, capital 'W' missing from 'Wordsworth'
line 2. comma missing after 'poet'
line 3. capital 'T' missing from 'There's', apostrophe missing from second 'there's'
line 4. replace full stop with a question mark after 'end'
line 5. full stop missing after Sun
corrections are shown in bold

2.

a.   across

b.   under

c.   beside

d.   through

e.   Underneath

Test 12

1.   *various options available such as: bough, cough, dough, rough, breakthrough*

2.
Nouns	**Adverbs**	**Prepositions**	**Adjectives**
young	rapidly	under	enormous
anger	slowly		young
elephant	always		
Sunday	under		

3.   b

95

4.

a. echoes

b. gateaux

c. lice

d. vertebrae

5. d

Test 13

1.

a. in

b. with

c. down, through

d. on, after

e. across

2. d

3.

a. past tense

b. future tense

c. past tense

d. present tense

e. present tense

f. present tense

4. Mortan's
missing apostrophe

5. door,
a comma is missing after the word 'door'

6. *no mistakes in line 6*

7. frightening:
the comma after 'frightening' should be a colon

8. *no mistakes in line 8*

9. Finlay
it should be a capital 'F'

Test 14

1.

a. seldom

b. imminent

c. deliberate

d. obey

e. comrade

f. forecast

g. vegetable

2.

a. were

b. threw

c. are

d. ate

e. drank

3. **Among** the birds of prey are the buzzards, which are **rather** like eagles but smaller and less powerful. The buzzard is larger than the **partridge**. They are found all over the world **except** in the Australian region. Only the common buzzard lives and nests in Great Britain. It is a **handsome** bird, dark brown above and usually barred brown and white below, with **bright** yellow legs and yellow on its curved bill. It has a **weak** mewing cry and a fine **soaring** flight.

    the passage has been rewritten with the correct spellings in bold

4. wife

Test 15

1. *a full stop is missing after the word 'run'*

2. They'd
    the apostrophe is missing from 'They'd' to show that it is a contraction of two words

3. *no mistakes in line 3*

4. Sometimes
    the letter 'S' should be capitalised

5. kingfishers
    the comma after kingfishers is unnecessary as stoats are clearly the last listed item

6. *no mistakes on line 6*

7. Ally's
    the apostrophe is missing from 'Ally's'

8. too
    should be 'too' rather than 'to' as Tom also wanted to run

9. they'd
    apostrophe missing from 'they'd' to show that it is a contraction of two words

10. c

11. I went to school with Tim, Sue and Craig went elsewhere.
    the comma should appear after 'Tom'

12. a

13. Ally and Tom are training for a marathon; they run together every other day.
    the semicolon should appear after the word 'marathon'

14. c

Test 16

1. *various examples are available such as:*

a. The calm lake was a mirror reflecting the scenery back.

b. Her tears were a river flowing down her cheeks.

c. The crocodile's teeth were white daggers.

d. The stormy ocean was a raging bull.

e. The field was a lake after the rain.

2. *various examples are available such as:*

a. co-ordinated
use a hyphen when the prefix ends with the same letter that starts the base word

b. self-service
use a hyphen after the following prefixes in most words: 'self', 'cross', 'all' and 'ex'

c. re-sign
use a hyphen to ensure the correct meaning is inferred, in this example something will be signed again, rather than inferring a resignation as in 'resign'

d. trans-Siberian
use a hyphen after prefixes preceding a number, a proper noun or an abbreviation

3.

a. "I'm **too** tired **to** walk home." the boy said.

b. **Two** girls travelled **to** the party.

c. James went **to** the shop **to** buy some milk.

d. It was **too** far **to** drive for just **two** days.

4. d

Test 17

1. **Sentences** should reflect the **severity** of the crime.

the misspelt words are shown corrected in bold

2. "**You'll** never guess what I've just seen**!**" said Thomas, excitedly.
    "What's that**?**" asked Henrietta**.**
    "Toby's **mum's** got a broomstick in the boot of her car. **Maybe** she's a witch!"
    "Don't be ridiculous! **We're** all going out for **Halloween** tonight**.**" replied Henrietta.
    "Oh yeah, I'd forgotten about that." said **Thomas.**

    line 1. missing apostrophe in 'you'll', missing exclamation mark and speech marks
    line 2. question mark missing after 'that', full stop missing after 'Henrietta'
    line 3. apostrophe missing from 'mum's', 'Maybe' is missing a capital 'M', speech marks missing after 'witch!'
    line 4. capital 'W' missing from 'we're', capital 'H' missing from Halloween, full stop required after 'tonight'
    line 5. capital 'T' required for 'Thomas', full stop at the end of the sentence

    missing punctuation is marked in bold

3. d

4. d

Test 18

1.
a.	revoke	b.	revive
c.	reverse	d.	resign
e.	reserve	f.	repent

2. must

3. c

4. c

5. as I was putting my socks on.

    this part of the sentence relies on the main clause to make sense

Test 19

1. He knew what his superpower would be: the ability to become invisible.

2. Meddling **M**eredith is angry and confused by claims that she is not co-operating with the FBI in its investigation into espionage. **A** senior US prosecutor complained on **M**onday that investigators working on the case were unable to contact Meredith at her home address.

    line 1. capital 'M' missing from 'Meredith', hyphen missing from 'co-operating'
    line 2. full stop missing after 'espionage', capital 'A' after the full stop
    line 3. capital 'M' on 'Monday'
    line 4. full stop after 'address'

    the corrections are shown in bold

3. c

4. downstairs

5.

a.	adjective	huge
b.	abstract noun	courage
c.	adverb	loudly
d.	pronoun	they
e.	conjunction	unless
f.	collective noun	set
g.	verb	hold

Test 20

1. A large **percentage** of the eggs sold in Britain are **battery**-produced. However, if you're lucky enough to live near to an old-**fashioned** farm, where the hens are free to **roam** about, you can **probably** get well-**flavoured** eggs with rich-coloured **yolks**.

   correct spellings are shown in bold

2. David had to **simplify** the directions so that they were easier to follow.

3. eyelashes

4.

a. disagree

b. unforgiving

c. inexcusable

d. mislead

e. intolerant

f. nonentity

5. "I will always love you," swooned Isabella. "Always."

6. *various options are available such as:*

a. The sun **was a ball of fire.**

b. The falling snowflakes **are dancers.**

c. Tobias is **a shining star.**

d. Her long hair **was a flowing golden river.**

Test 21

1. "I have exciting news." whispered Shirley.

2. Kathleen was **desperate** to **achieve** a trophy for her sculpture, but there was no **guarantee** that she **would**. In her **experience** the sculptors that produced the largest **pieces** usually gained the **necessary** points for a trophy. But she held out hope for this year's **annual** competition; she really didn't want to **lose** again.
   spelling corrections are shown in bold

3. "The **biscuits** are for **Wendy's mum's** dog—you mustn't eat them**!**"
   remove the apostrophe from 'biscuits', add apostrophes to 'Wendy's' and 'mum's', add an exclamation mark at the end of the sentence, close the speech marks at the end

4. The invitation stated, "You are   **cordially**   invited to the party."

5. c

Test 22

1. c

2. The biscuits I found in the cupboard were **mine**. Jake thought they were **his**, but I knew **his** were chocolate chip.

3. some, an, her

4.

a. shan't

b. wouldn't

c. I'd

d. didn't

e. they'd

5. To make delicious muffins you need:

- Flour
- Two eggs
- Butter
- Sugar
- Vanilla extract
- Blueberries

6. Jack Taylor, last year's winner, is trailing by two points.

7.

a. change

b. manufacture

c. dig

d. amateur

Test 23

1. A smart, professional businessman in a grey suit

2. who scored the winning goal

3. on

4. It was a credit to the staff that the students had low levels of **anxiety** in the lead-up to the tests. The importance of preparation had been instilled in the children as its positive **effect** cannot be **exaggerated**. After an **exhaustive** search on the internet for a venue for the exams, a **suitable** location was found. Afterwards, the staff were **justifiably** proud of the children's achievements.
   correctly spelt words are shown in bold

Test 24

1. eight, charming, Victorian, silver

2. passive
   the boys (the subject) had something done to them (being chased)

3. a

4.

a. conspiracy

b. sobering

c. perceived

d. foes

e. shunning

5. c

6. a

7.

a. "You must **have** seen it!" exclaimed Mark, "It was enormous!"

b. **They're** getting nothing until Wednesday.
   or
   They are getting nothing until Wednesday.

   'ain't getting nothing' would be a double negative

c. We **were** really late for school and my teacher **wasn't** happy.

Test 25

1. scarcity

2.

a. premonition b. pretext
c. prominent d. promontory
e. promotion f. prosperous

3.

a. decided
b. annually
c. delay

4.

a. as
b. because
c. until

5.

a. ejection
b. dilation
c. adaption
d. fixation

6.   c

Test 26

1. **Stagger**

   a. to walk about unsteadily

   b. to arrange things in a zigzag formation

   Enterprise

   a. a project or undertaking

   b. a business or company

2.
   a. Jason whispered, "I'm coming now."

   b. "Are we there yet?" the children whined.

   c. "It's time you were both in bed." said Sarah, the babysitter.

   d. At university, Jane specialised in three subjects: Latin, German and French.

3. Winter heliotrope produces its clusters of **vanilla**-scented, pale **purple** flowers from January to April. A **valuable** early nectar **source** for pollinating insects, the blooms are **followed** by a **carpet** of kidney-shaped leaves.

   the misspelt words are shown corrected in bold

4. quizzes

5. species

Test 27

1. "Where are you going on holiday this year?" enquired Susan.
   "To India." replied Cora.
   "I haven't been there. I'd love to go!" exclaimed Susan.
   "You should!" Cora laughed.

2. sited

3. poultry

4. tiring

5. lent

6. Annabel sailed out of the **harbour, aboard** the **yacht**. Today she would be sailing **entirely** alone, and she was **tremendously** excited. The **whole fleet** had sailed together on **Wednesday**, but today she had the sea to herself. She **seized** the helm and steered the boat to the left as she **suspected** the wind would be in her **favour** if she went in that direction.

   the misspelt words are shown corrected in bold

Test 28

1.
   a. miscellaneous
   b. harmonious
   c. envious
   d. infectious
   e. courageous
   f. fibrous

2. c

3. torpedoes

4. Cheshire is **an** English county with a short coastline on the Irish Sea. It **is** bordered by seven other counties. The River Mersey forms the northern boundary **with** Lancashire, and the county touches the corner **of** Yorkshire in the northeast. Shropshire is the boundary **on** the south.

the correct words are shown in bold

Test 29

1. d

2. a

3.
a. active
b. passive
c. active
d. active
e. passive

4. awkward

5. accommodate

6. *there are no spelling mistakes in this line*

7. attached

8. sufficient

9. According

10. there
    instead of 'their' at the beginning of the sentence

11. resign

Test 30

1. c

2. The balloon burst with a loud bang.
   n. balloon, v. burst, adj. loud
   other sentences are acceptable as long as you have a noun, a verb and an adjective

3. c

4. The glistening snow

5. I'd love to see their new house.

6. kangaroos

7. centrally, justice, cartridge, uphold, rampage, cabin

Test 31

1. crises

2. An Italian lady taught Sanjay to cook.

3.
    a. normal
    b. mature
    c. behave
    d. happy
    e. lingual
    f. collapse

4.
    a. WWF
    b. NZ
    c. PO
    d. MB
    e. PC

5. c

115

Test 32

1.
We are looking for volunteers from the community to join us in enhancing the opportunities and experiences of Valley Park Primary School**'**s children. There are various ways in which you could help**:** as a paired teacher**;** as a sports coach or referee; as a chaperone on outings; or by sharing a specialist knowledge you have. The paired reading scheme operates every morning from 9.00 - 9.30am. **H**elpers elect to come as many mornings as they feel able and full training is given. Pupils**'** responses have been wholly positive**.** **O**ne pupil recently said, "I thought I'd never be able to read. But thanks to Mr Po, who**'**s been helping me for three months**,** I**'**ve just read 'Harry Potter and the Philosopher's Stone' all on my own."

  line 2. apostrophe missing from 'School's'
  line 3 . colon missing after 'help', semicolon missing after 'teacher'
  line 4. semicolon missing after 'referee' and 'outings'
  line 5. capital 'H' in 'Helpers'
  line 6. apostrophe missing after 'Pupils"
  line 7. full stop after 'positive', capital 'O' in 'One'
  line 8. apostrophe missing from 'who's', comma missing after 'months', apostrophe missing from 'I've'

  corrections are shown in the extract in bold

2.   clamour, theme, headdress, door, herring, bathe

Printed in Great Britain
by Amazon